Get the Life You Really Want

James Caan

PORTFOLIO
PENGUIN

PORTFOLIO PENGUIN

Published by the Penguin Group
Penguin Books Ltd, 80 Strand, London WC2R 0RL, England
Penguin Group (USA) Inc., 375 Hudson Street, New York, New York 10014, USA
Penguin Group (Canada), 90 Eglinton Avenue East, Suite 700, Toronto, Ontario,
Canada M4P 2Y3 (a division of Pearson Penguin Canada Inc.)
Penguin Ireland, 25 St Stephen's Green, Dublin 2, Ireland
(a division of Penguin Books Ltd)
Penguin Group (Australia), 250 Camberwell Road, Camberwell, Victoria 3124,
Australia (a division of Pearson Australia Group Pty Ltd)
Penguin Books India Pvt Ltd, 11 Community Centre,
Panchsheel Park, New Delhi – 110 017, India
Penguin Group (NZ), 67 Apollo Drive, Rosedale, Auckland 0632, New Zealand
(a division of Pearson New Zealand Ltd)
Penguin Books (South Africa) (Pty) Ltd, 24 Sturdee Avenue,
Rosebank, Johannesburg 2196, South Africa

Penguin Books Ltd, Registered Offices: 80 Strand, London WC2R 0RL, England

www.penguin.com

First published 2012
1

Copyright © James Caan, 2012
All rights reserved

The moral right of the author has been asserted

Set in 12/16 pt Stone Serif
Typeset by Jouve (UK), Milton Keynes
Printed in Great Britain by Clays Ltd, St Ives plc

ISBN: 978–0–241–95878–0

www.greenpenguin.co.uk

MIX
Paper from
responsible sources
FSC
www.fsc.org   FSC™ C018179

Penguin Books is committed to a sustainable
future for our business, our readers and our
planet. This book is made from paper certified
by the Forest Stewardship Council.

Contents

Introduction

Taking charge of your life

A couple of years ago I met a young woman called Gina. She had recently spent some time in prison, and after her release it seemed no one was willing to help her. Gina found it impossible to get a job because of her criminal record. Yet although the odds were stacked against her, she wouldn't give up. She was absolutely determined to change her life and support her young family.

She made contact with the Prince's Trust. This is the charity which gives practical support to young people who are finding life challenging and helps them to rebuild their lives. The Trust approached me and asked me to see if there was any way I could help Gina, as she was so committed to turning things around. We met up, and got on really well from the start.

Gina had started a flower-arranging business called Blooming Scent. She was creating beautiful floral pieces for events like christenings and wedding receptions. So together we looked at how she could make her new business work. In particular we thought about the way she organized her time and how she could get more business from her regular customers.

A few months later, I found myself sitting in Buckingham Palace. Prince Charles had organized a black-tie dinner, an event called Invest in Futures, to raise funds for the Trust. I was amazed to be there myself, in such splendid surroundings. But I was even more amazed by Gina.

Gina stood up in front of everybody at that dinner, an audience which included royalty, cabinet ministers and celebrities. She told them – simply and honestly – how she had succeeded in changing her life. It was an inspiring and very moving speech.

I felt immensely proud of Gina, and I was happy to have played some small part in getting her there. Of course, the drive to succeed and to change her life had come from within her. I had just guided her energy.

I also saw something of myself in Gina. I'm often surprised that people who meet me think, for some reason, that I must have had an easy life, that I had things handed to me on a plate. They, in turn, are surprised when they discover that I actually left school, and home, at sixteen.

I left against the wishes of my parents and I made some difficult choices. I didn't go to college or university, but started working straight away. During my late teens and early twenties I re-invented myself. I learnt on the job and from being exposed to real life.

Then I decided to set up my first business, a recruitment company. I did not have much experience but I had plenty of cheek and self-belief.

A lot of that self-belief was directly connected to the excitement of the first deal I ever made, aged twelve. I remember it clearly. My father used to own a business where he made leather garments. I took one of his new leather jackets and paraded it round the playground at school, making sure the jacket got noticed, and then sold it. I realized that I had made more money from selling one jacket than my father gave me as pocket money for the entire month. The excitement and thrill of doing that deal have never left me.

As I got older and a little bit wiser, I realized that although I had rejected my parents' advice – my father wanted me to take over his business and I didn't want to – my dad had taught me many great things. There's one piece of advice he gave me that I still believe in completely. If you ask the right questions, the right decisions will make themselves.

Making big changes in your life is always a daunting prospect. It is much easier to do nothing. Sticking with the life you know is comfortable, even if you are not completely happy with it.

But if you go ahead and make changes, the feeling of freedom is truly exciting. Suddenly you are in charge of your own destiny. You're no longer playing a bit part in someone else's dream.

This book is full of ideas based on my thirty years of experience as an entrepreneur. They are the things I have learnt from setting up and running successful businesses. Together they make up what I call the *entrepreneurial spirit*. This is a way of approaching and thinking about the world that makes change really happen.

By 'entrepreneurial' I don't just mean setting up a business. It could equally be about deciding to change your career, or getting a community project off the ground, or putting a band together. It's all about taking charge of your own decisions and being able to shape your own future.

The great thing is there are no boundaries to being an entrepreneur. You can be fourteen, or eighty-four. You can be male or female, married or single. You can work on your own or as part of a team. The entrepreneurial spirit empowers. It can transform every part of life.

I hope you can apply these ideas to transforming yourself. And that, like Gina, you will have the determination and the confidence to re-invent your life. Use these ideas to add value to everything you do. They will help improve the chances of you achieving your own goals.

1

Release Your Potential

Why do you want to change?

I am a great believer in what I call the Power of
Why. It's amazing how a change to your state
of mind can start to unleash your potential
right away. This is all about understanding
what is important to you, what is spurring you
onwards and upwards. It is finding the part of
your personality that will give you the energy
and the power to transform your life.

The Power of Why is something I am always
looking for when I think about backing a new
business. It was what I tried to uncover whenever I was sitting in the Dragons' Den. During
each presentation I studied the person making
the pitch. I always back people, rather than
purely ideas, so I want to know what is driving
them on.

I invest in the person leading the business. If
I don't feel their passion, then it doesn't matter
to me how good their financial plan is. I won't

be convinced they will achieve what they are forecasting.

I want to identify what it is in their make-up that tells me they have the determination to succeed. How will they deal with the problems they are certain to come up against? Will they go that extra mile to make it?

Everybody has their own reasons for wanting to achieve their goals. Mostly people will say that they are doing it for themselves. However, one of the great motivators is the fact you want to change for other people.

I know this goes against the grain of usual business advice. You will often be told you should be changing your life for you, and not for other people. However, I think that is too simple a response. Of course we all want to change for ourselves. But the problem is that if it is *only* for ourselves we want to change, we too easily accept compromises. Our pain threshold is much lower. We will always cut ourselves more slack. But let's say your mum and your brother have each put some of their own money into your latest venture. Believe me, you will work twice as hard to make sure you don't let them down.

It's like Gina, who wanted to turn her life around after being in prison. She wanted to do that not only to support her young kids, but also to show her family and friends that she had changed. 'Now I can look my family in the eye,' she said, 'instead of hanging my head in shame.'

Dig down and find not only *what* it is in your life but *who* you want to change for. That is a powerful force. The more factors you can add to make your commitment to your journey stronger, the more likely you are to achieve your goals.

My dad left his life in Pakistan and travelled over to England without a word of English. He did that because he wanted to provide for me and his other children. Can you imagine what it must have been like for him arriving here? Somehow after arriving in London he made his way to the East End. He relied on nothing but an address on a piece of paper and a lot of pointing and smiling. Again, what determination. He was so driven, so motivated, so committed to being successful in business. That character – his DNA – is part of me.

The very first investment I ever made on *Dragons' Den* was in a person rather than a product. Sammy French came in with her Fit Fur Life treadmill for dogs. It wasn't the idea of the dog treadmills themselves that convinced me. I knew absolutely nothing about them or their market potential.

What inspired me was Sammy's own story. Here was a single mum, living in a council flat, working as a waitress to pay the bills. She was selling her treadmills in the evening because she really wanted to earn more money to give one of her daughters a private education. That was driving her on.

As well as that sense of motivation, which gives you the desire and the hunger to transform your life, you also need the willingness to start out on this process of change. You have to do that without necessarily knowing where you will end up.

It is what I try and use when I help other people in their businesses. I hope to come in and give them confidence. I want them to believe in the fact that they can achieve what they want. That is another massive part of giving yourself the right mindset to change your life.

When I tell people they will be successful, I start the process of them believing in themselves. I may not have done anything practical or specific. Often I have helped them with the why, rather than the how. I might simply have had a conversation with them, but the key thing I have done is to remove the fear of failure that is dragging them back. I want to get rid of the voice in their head saying, 'You can't do it, you're useless, you haven't got the experience.'

Everyone knows that fear of failure. The common ingredient shared by every successful entrepreneur I meet is that they have learnt to deal with the threat of failure.

I was once at a conference with Bill Gates, and he was asked whether he ever doubted he would succeed. He said of course he had. When he started Microsoft, it nearly got stuck at the first hurdle because he couldn't get a company car for the first salesman he hired. The car leasing firm refused, point blank. They had never heard of Microsoft, the company had no track record, they would never make it. If a friend of Bill's had not agreed to guarantee the lease, the Microsoft story would have ended there and then. Bill Gates learnt not to be fazed by the fear of failure.

Top sportsmen and women do the same. When Wayne Rooney finds himself in sight of the goal with the ball at his feet, he is fearless. He will just take the shot. He believes he *can* score, even if that time he shoots wide. Yet over and over again you see other players miss a tap-in, in front of an open goal. They fumble the shot. Why? They feel the pressure. The adrenalin is pumping and they start worrying about the possibility of missing. Sure enough, they miss. They've lost their nerve.

Great players in any sport have harnessed their fear of failure. They have learnt how to draw on their belief and their confidence, and importantly they are able to do that on the big points.

I find the same in business. The basic skills are the same. There are people with all the business skills you need who still fail. It is all locked up in that emotional thought, 'I can't do it.' Those who succeed say, 'Yes. I can do this. And I will.'

Mindset: the JC approach

- Find out what it is inside you that is going to drive you on to transform your life. Those driving forces are all-powerful. They will encourage you to overcome the natural, human fear of change and fear of failure.

- If you can work out who the people are that you really want to demonstrate your transformed life to, that is a great additional motivation.

- The difference lies not in the basic skills we all have. It is in our minds. It is in the confidence that we can get what we want.

- **It is your mindset, not your ability, that shapes how high you will go. In other words, it is your attitude, not your aptitude, that determines your altitude.**

2

Resolutions

Setting your targets and priorities

Every time New Year comes around, the same thing happens. We sit down and decide to turn over a new leaf. Then we draw up a list of all the resolutions we intend to keep for the next twelve months.

It's nearly always the same list, isn't it? We're definitely going to lose weight and join the local gym so we can feel fitter. We will eat healthier food, give up smoking, drink less. We are going to look for a new job because the one we're in seems boring and predictable.

And what happens? We end up with lists of what are unrealistic aims. They are targets that look great on paper, but after a couple of weeks they sound far too difficult. The list of resolutions goes in the waste-paper bin. Never mind, leave it for another year. It's not a very motivating activity.

If you really want to change your life, thinking about your plans and ambitions once a year on 1 January is not enough. I firmly believe that planning what you want to achieve should be a year-round activity.

Life is fluid, events happen, contexts change. So my brain is always ticking over, reflecting and analysing the things that are happening in my life, both at work and outside. Each day I am asking myself questions, testing myself. How can I improve what I am doing? How can I change things for the better?

Asking questions and working out what needs changing is great. But then you have to move from *thinking* about things to actually *doing* them. To start moving forwards and get some traction, it is important to set targets. Otherwise you go through life like a pinball, being bounced around by other people telling you what to do.

Unlike those New Year's resolutions it is important to set targets that are achievable. So many people set goals but never achieve them. They choose hopes and aspirations that remain just that: hopeful and aspirational. In other words, don't aim for the stars straight away. Otherwise you might just end up clutching at thin air.

To me goals and targets first have to be attainable. As well as aiming for large targets, you should build in milestones along the way. Break down the big goal into bite-sized chunks that you can see, touch, smell, feel. These smaller steps make it far more likely that you will reach the end of the journey. They allow you to look ahead, see a clear path, and enjoy some success really quite quickly.

Each step has to be something you can achieve quite easily. If you set the next milestone too far down the road, your motivation quickly weakens because you know you can't get there in the immediate future.

When I started out in my first business I had no idea where it might lead me. Of course I wanted to be successful at what I was doing, but I didn't have some master plan. I hadn't seen myself ending up running a private equity business and appearing on TV. My first milestone was really quite simple. When I set up my recruitment business I had an office which had no windows. It was little more than a broom cupboard, with a desk, a chair and a phone. I felt like I was working in a cell; it was really bad for my morale.

So the only thing I was obsessed with was making enough money to rent an office with a window. I plugged away, started finding a few clients and landing some deals, and I made enough money to move to an office with a window. As soon as I got that office I set myself another small goal: to hire somebody else to work with me. It was lonely being a one-man band. Cooped up in an office every day with only myself for company was driving me mad. I wanted to work with someone so I could enjoy sharing the successes with them.

I still didn't have a private meeting room for interviews and client meetings, though. I was having to use hotel lobbies and coffee shops. So that was my next target. Then I aimed for sales of £10,000 a month. When I got there, I wondered if we could do £20,000 a month. Even twenty-five years later I can tell you every single step of the way.

At each stage I thought of something I could achieve that would drive me on. I fixed on something that was measurable and would make my life better.

It's like when a friend suggests you might want to join them to run a marathon for charity. Let's say the charity is one you are really keen to support. However, it won't work if they try to convince you by saying, 'Come on, do you want to run twenty-six and a bit miles next

April?' If it was me, I know I would not say yes. I would be out straight away, because the distance sounds just too far, too big a target, too unachievable. I am not even going to bother.

But if the same friend comes to me and says, 'James, I'm doing some running to get fit. Do you fancy coming with me to jog for a couple of miles round the park?' I'm OK with that. Then a week later he comes back and says, 'How about another run? This time let's just take it easy and go over to the West End and back?' Great. It all sounds do-able.

All I need is a few milestones to help me along the journey. We build up the amount of running, almost without knowing it, to taking part in a ten-kilometre run at some point. Before I know it we are feeling quite good about moving up another gear. Now, when I think about the possibility of doing a marathon, those twenty-six-plus miles don't seem like that big a stretch.

Here's another example. I have always loved cars. I always wanted to drive a Rolls-Royce Phantom, which was probably the most expensive car I could have imagined. When I started out, though, my target wasn't to own a Phantom. My target was to have a Chopper bike, which was the dream mode of transport for any kid growing up in the early 70s.

I started doing a paper round and saved enough to buy a Chopper. After a while I set my sights on a racing bike. Then from a racing bike I went to a moped and from a moped I went to a 50cc motorbike before moving up to a 250cc bike.

In one of my first jobs I kept enough money back to buy my first car, a little MG Midget. Then I had to take my driving test: I'd got the car, but not the licence! If I look back at that particular journey I realize my targets were quite realistic and very achievable (and yes, in the end, I did get that Rolls-Royce Phantom).

The big difference with using milestones rather than huge targets is that whenever you encounter a problem or a setback you only fall back to the last milestone you reached. In everything I have ever done I have gone from step to step. I am almost fearful of jumping too many steps at one go because, without knowing it, I think that there's a risk. If you try and jump too far, you run the risk of falling a long way back.

It is inevitable you will drop back at some point, because in life things tend not to go exactly to plan. The good thing is that with milestones in place you won't fall right back to the beginning.

That's why I have planned my life in manageable steps. There have been many situations where I have jumped a few milestones but equally there have been plenty where I have slipped back a few. But so far I have never dropped back to the bottom.

Targets: the JC approach

- You need targets to move forwards and achieve the change you want. But if you only set one huge target you'll find it really difficult to get started and overcome natural lack of progress.

- Try to get the balance right between positive ambitions and what is realistic. You want to feel forward movement, not frustration.

- Make sure there are short gaps between each of your milestones. Then you can see where you are going.

- **Always relish the pleasure of making it to your next milestone.**

3

Reclaim the Day

Managing your time

The kind of computer power that once used to fill a room now fits into our phones. We have reduced the time it takes to communicate. We can phone each other round the world instantly. Yet despite all the time-saving devices we have, we haven't managed to add any more hours to the day.

There are still only twenty-four hours in each day. Still only seven days in each week. We are constantly being harassed by work deadlines. We can often feel bombarded by e-mails and texts, let alone trying to fit in our family and social life.

I know my own time is increasingly stretched. The one thing I never have is enough time. Time is the most precious thing we have. Every day, including Saturdays and most Sundays, I have meetings from first thing in the morning through to the evening.

I realized this when my daughter Jemma said, 'Dad, this is weird. We live in the same house, and yet we can have a whole week when none of us see each other.'

She wasn't exaggerating. It was true. My average day is quite ridiculous. I now manage over forty companies. I deal with forty chief executives. I start at 6 a.m. and check and respond to e-mails up until 8 a.m. Then it's meetings throughout the day, which is split into fifteen-minute blocks in a diary that is booked five to six months in advance.

So although I spoke to Jemma on the phone every day, we didn't get much genuine one-on-one time. I had work commitments all day and usually a business event in the evening. My daughter has her own busy work and social life. We were easily capable of going through an entire week not seeing each other.

Jemma's comment made me think about the practical ways you can de-clutter your life. How can you make space to think about what you want to do and then do it?

For me, the simple answer is deciding between what is essential and what is simply 'nice to have'. Time management is about looking at your diary every morning. Ask yourself whether each task or activity is crucial and critical to what you are doing. This is especially important when you are in the middle of trying to change your life.

'Critical' in this context doesn't always have to be ticking off something on the 'to do' list. Critical could be making time for the family as much as arranging another meeting.

I work hard to try and make my time work hard for me, especially when I am travelling. The other day I had to go to a meeting in the City of London. The meeting was a forty-five-minute car journey from my office. Amelia, who manages my diary, knew there were three people who wanted to talk to me that morning. It was impossible to see them in person, and I physically didn't have any gaps in the diary.

But I did have those forty-five minutes. So Amelia called each of the people who wanted meetings. She said, 'I know you really want to speak to James. Would you be happy to do a fifteen-minute conference call while he's in the car?' Between us we managed to fit those three 'meetings' into the one car journey.

Careful time management is absolutely crucial for me. I am always being asked to do more than I can possibly cram into my day. So every day appears to be bursting at the seams. Most people don't value their time enough. I aim to maximize the value of every second of my day. I am very careful about allocating time for everything I need to do. That includes time to go jogging in the park, time to have a massage. It's all scheduled in.

Even when I have down time, I try to use it wisely. In my personal life, when I am away with my family on holiday, I get up early because I am incapable of lying in. I will be thinking about things, doodling ideas. Then between 9 and 11 each morning we have break-fast as a family. The next couple of hours after that are down time before lunch.

I am not that keen on lounging by the pool. It's not in my character. I remember having a chat once with my wife, Aisha, about this. I said, 'Darling, if you were going to be on the beach having a swim and I was sitting there reading a book, you'd be fine with that, wouldn't you?'

'Of course,' she said.

'So in that case would you mind if I was on the iPad or my Blackberry rather than reading a book? I want to keep in touch with my busi-ness. For you, having a swim or reading, that's what you enjoy. That's your chilling-out time. But I am quite happy to be on the Blackberry.'

So we agreed that in those couple of hours

between 11 and 1, I could do some work. The same applied between 3 and 5 in the afternoon. We'd have more family time at lunch. The whole evening was for us to have dinner together before taking a walk or going to a show.

It works really well. My office knows they can organize calls and batch e-mails for me to answer. It doesn't affect my wife or my children because it is controlled. If we decide we actually want go out all day together, I will simply cancel the work slot.

I generally find that in a week away I can do several hours' work on four of the seven days. It means there is never a situation at work where something can't move forward because I am not in the office. As an entrepreneur in business that is really important. The deals and the discussions don't stop for my holidays. However, I can also have plenty of fun with the family.

Once you start thinking about organizing your time like that you can apply it every day. It becomes second nature. So when Jemma made me realize we weren't seeing each other enough, we changed things around. We said, 'Let's agree that, whatever else happens, every fortnight we have dinner together.'

So that's what we do. Dinner is in the diary

every other Wednesday. I will never try and change it. The girls pick a restaurant and Aisha and I will be there at 8.30 sharp. Guess what? It is one of the highlights of my week.

But – and this is an important but – planning your time doesn't mean you can't be flexible. In fact, just the opposite. Clearly you can't plan for the unexpected. It doesn't fit into the diary. So when the unexpected happens you have to look at your priorities. What you thought was the most important thing in your day is no longer so. Something else is now more of a priority: you simply re-schedule. It's about good decision-making.

The structure I have set up allows me to get the best from a day, but it can all be changed. I review my schedule every Monday, and first thing every morning.

If I wake up one morning with a touch of flu and have to stay in bed to recover, these things happen. For the next two or three days I'll have to cancel everything. It's not the end of the world.

I realize that I am fortunate to be able to plan from first thing in the morning to the end of the evening. My daughters are adults now: I don't have to ferry them to and fro. Yet, even if your time is constrained by school runs and after-school clubs, you can block out the time that you do have available. Maybe you can set aside a four-hour block each day from 9 a.m. to 1 p.m. or 11 a.m. to 3 p.m.? Take those four hours and slice them up so you are twice as effective, and you will do as much as somebody dawdling through an eight-hour day.

Time: the JC approach

- Managing time is all about working out how *you* can be in control of your time, not the other way around. You are in charge.

- Remember the difference between what is critical and what is 'nice to have'. Reduce the amount of time spent on the 'nice to have' and you will become more efficient.

- Don't forget to make sure you are building in time to enjoy yourself, time to relax with the kids. It is just as crucial to your well-being. Build it in to your diary and stick to it.

- If something unexpected crops up, re-think your plans. You want your time

21

management to be flexible, not a straitjacket.

- **Value your time, and it will become your most valuable asset.**

4

Reaching Out

Sharing your plans

Let me tell you a story about my younger sister, Nazima. One Sunday afternoon I popped over to see her for a catch-up about what we were both doing. She had made some tea and put a plate of samosas on the table for us to share.

Now I love samosas. I *really* love samosas. I tried a few of hers and said, 'Nisa, I've had loads of samosas, but these are delicious. Why don't you make some more and sell them to your friends?'

'Do you think they're that good?' she asked.

'Actually, I do.'

The next weekend she spent some time cooking in her kitchen and made 250 samosas. On Monday morning she went off on the school run with a few of them in her bag. She asked the other mums she knew to taste them to see if they'd like to buy some. By the end of that first day she had sold out her 250 samosas.

The following Sunday, Nazima got up a little

bit earlier and made 500 samosas. The same thing happened. She did the school run, but this time she also got on her phone. She rang the rest of our family and some of her other friends. Lo and behold, she sold all 500.

When I next saw her, she told me she'd got one of the other mums involved to give her a hand. Between them they were now turning out around 1,000 samosas a week. I was astonished and thrilled for her. 'Are you kidding me? How are you making them?'

'Well,' she said, 'we spend all day Sunday together making them, but it's really good. I'm having fun. I'm enjoying it.'

Nazima had just proved to me the power of networking. She had talked to the other mums on the school run. They had bought her samosas. One of them had volunteered to join in. She had followed her instinct and understood about unleashing the power of other people to help her.

You can only unleash all that power by talking to people. Don't keep all your thoughts and ambitions to yourself. Tell other people what you are hoping for and what you are trying to achieve. Share your plans.

Maybe you are trying to launch a charity to help your local community. Perhaps you're looking for somebody who can give you some specific training. Or, like Nazima, you have a product or service you think you can sell. You'll be amazed how often somebody you know from the school run, or who you meet at a party, knows the very person who can help.

There is no need to change your life all by yourself. Yes, you are the person who will be providing the energy and the drive. You will have dug down and found the trigger to move you onwards and upwards. That doesn't mean it has to be a one-man or one-woman job.

Whenever I work with new businesses, one of the things I tell them is to go and talk to other people about what they are doing. They often don't believe me, especially the ones who think they've invented the next cat's-eye or iPod. They want to keep it secret. They think that by sharing they are going to let somebody steal their idea. They get obsessed by sorting out patents and letters of agreement. Frankly, I think that level of secrecy is over-valued. In fact, it's often counter-productive.

I understand *why* they think that, but I think they are kidding themselves. I ask them to ask themselves just how good an idea it can be if somebody could reproduce it after a five-minute chat. The answer is that it can't be that unique if it's so easy to copy.

The other key point is that if you are very close to an idea, it's easy to miss the problem, the critical flaw, in it. Since other people are generally going to have some distance and be more objective, they are very good at putting their finger on something you've missed.

This was something else I learnt from my dad. I upset him hugely when I decided not to go into the family business and do my own thing instead. Yet he still gave me the best advice he could, quietly and patiently. As time went on I realized how smart he was. He would spend time sitting, watching, listening and taking things in. He taught me that if I wanted to improve any idea I had, I should talk to other people and ask them for their feedback.

So I always talk about my ideas with as many people as possible. When I come away from a conversation or a meeting, I have always picked up some new piece of information. I have usually had my eyes opened to a completely different angle.

It has always been one of my strengths to recognize my weaknesses. I know I am good at certain things, not so good at others. Another of my skills has been working out how to find somebody who knows how to hang a picture on a wall far better than I could ever do.

You can do this in a less random, more structured way too. There are networking groups, self-help organizations and websites talking about the part of your life you particularly want to change.

When attending a networking event I'm often amazed by how many people don't seem to want to grasp the opportunity to network. I'm not sure what they hope to achieve by hovering on the fringes and not actually having a conversation with anybody. Be proactive, open up, engage – and remember to listen as much as you talk. It should be a 50:50 balance. You'll come away on a high, boosted by the number of people who want to help you.

However, don't ignore or neglect your old or current networks in the excitement of making new contacts. It is always easier to draw on existing contacts than to build new ones.

Sharing ideas: the JC approach

- You don't have to change your life all by yourself. In fact, involving other people and telling them your plans will be life-changing in itself.

27

- Always look for feedback. You usually come away from any conversation with one extra piece of advice or idea that you didn't have before. It could be the one that makes all the difference.

- When you go to any kind of networking event, don't forget to network. There's no value in sitting there being shy. Get out there and talk about what you want to achieve.

- The more you talk to people, the more questions you ask, the better informed and the stronger you are going to be – but listen just as much as you talk.

- **Use every single one of your networks, old and new: they will all reinforce Team You.**

5

Ready Reckoning

Thinking about money

In difficult financial times, one of the greatest sources of stress is money or, more usually, the lack of it. By applying some basic business thinking, you can start freeing yourself from those mental pressures.

Remember my sister Nazima. There she was producing her 1,000 samosas a week. On my next visit to see her I had to have a few more, just to check on quality control. They were still delicious.

I suggested she should think about turning her cooking hobby into a proper business. 'Why don't you find yourself a small industrial unit? You could hire some more people to help you,' I said.

'No, no, James,' she protested. 'I'm not a businesswoman, I'm a mum with three kids. I can't do this. You're freaking me out! I don't know anything about business and finance. That's what *you're* good at.'

So I asked her to think about how she organized her household bills. She had the mortgage to pay, the electricity and gas, shopping bills.

'You've got a mortgage on your house. So now we're going to call that the rent for the industrial unit. You go to the shops to buy your groceries. Well, now you are going to go to a wholesaler. You are going to buy exactly the same groceries, only more of them. That is called your cost of sales.

'At the moment you set aside money for your kids, for all their bits and pieces. In a business that's going to be the money for your staff . . . There is no major difference.'

She wasn't at all convinced. 'James, you are over-simplifying it. It can't be that easy. I don't know how to make a profit.'

'Let's think about that,' I said. 'Right now, if you need a little extra money for a new sofa, you cut back on something. You say, "I won't go out to a restaurant this week, or I'll wait to get that coat I've seen." You trim your costs.

'In a business all you have to do is make sure that your income is more than your costs are. If it isn't, you have to reduce part of your costs. It is exactly the same principle.'

If you can run and manage a household, you have got all the basic skills for running a business. If you apply those basics you can run a household, or a business, much more efficiently.

The other day I was sitting in a half-day meeting called the Chief Executives' Forum. It's something we do in my company Hamilton Bradshaw every year. We invite all the chief executives within the group to come in. I asked each of them what their key challenges were.

One of the guys spoke up. 'You know, I have to confess I am not really that financially minded. I have a great finance director, but he always makes me feel a bit inadequate.'

'That's a really great point,' I said. 'Because of *Dragons' Den*, everyone thinks I must be brilliant at finance. But look at my background. I left school at sixteen. I didn't go to university. I'm not an accountant, not a banker. I have no financial education of any description at all. The truth is that I'm not particularly good with numbers. I've never run a profit and loss account. I don't know how to use Excel spreadsheets. Everyone on my staff can produce a better spreadsheet than me.

'Yet the public believe that I am very good at numbers and business. So how can I run a multi-million-pound business if I don't understand those things? I'll tell you honestly that what I am actually good at is adding up and taking away. Good old sums. I understand debits and credits.'

I told them exactly what I had told Nazima. I used a whiteboard and gave them the same story. Money comes in and then we have costs. We plan and we budget. If we get something left we call it profit, and if we don't it's called a loss. 'Now,' I asked them all, 'tell me what the difference is.'

They were all looking at me in puzzled astonishment. 'Yes, James, but what about budgeting for one-off items or the time of the year?'

'OK. At home a one-off item is the fridge going wrong or the car needing a new clutch. And the time of the year – seasonality – means planning for birthdays or holidays once a year. It's the same thing.'

All that the bookkeepers, accountants and financial advisers will do is present that as a more complex spreadsheet. And what I find strange is that I have worked with chartered accountants, people who have business degrees or have worked at major accountancy firms for years, and yet I can still find holes in what they do. How come? I think they get so involved in the detail that they forget the principle of common sense.

I am never afraid of asking really basic questions. So when I do talk to accountants, I ask them, 'Which box does that go in? Is that in the income box or the cost box?' There are only three boxes. You've got income, you've got cost and the third box is profit. There isn't a fourth box. If the basics don't work, the rest of it doesn't matter. That formula has never left me, and believe me, it works. Stick to the core, to what is fundamental.

I believe that's why I can often be more effective, more efficient. I keep it simple. I get to the point more quickly. Instead of spending a month producing thirty pages of printout, I use one piece of paper. I sketch out the essential elements on a side of A4.

It makes it so much easier to spot the problems. Once you identify the problems, you can start doing something about them. In difficult economic times, people start worrying about money issues, which is only natural. But they are wasting the emotional energy they should be using to go back to the basics and sort out any financial problems.

I have been in all of those situations: running out of cash, not having enough money to pay bills, the VAT and other taxes. My attitude is always to remain calm, because there will be a solution, but only if you talk to people. I've talked to clients who owe me money that is not due for another month, but I tell them I need the money now: 'Is there any way you can pay me earlier?' I have even asked to be paid on account although the work is not yet finished.

There are many businesses that have gone under because they were too embarrassed to ask. There is no point in being heroic and noble and going bust. As always, I say turn every situation to your advantage. Turn the traditional mindset on its head, observe what everybody else is doing and do the opposite.

Financials: the JC approach

- Apply the essential rules of housekeeping. Money comes in, costs go out, and you are left with a profit or a loss. Adjusting the costs is the way to budget.

- Don't let the accountants, bankers or financial advisers bamboozle you. It is very easy to lose sight of those basics behind loads of jargon and sheets of figures.

- If you are having a conversation about money and don't understand what you are being told, ask questions.

- **With finance, keep it simple, keep calm and you will start to keep in control.**

6

Refresh Your Career

Taking a new direction

An obvious way to change your life is to think, 'I need to get a new job.' The work you are doing on a day-to-day basis can easily feel dull and uninspiring. You feel you are stuck in a rut. If you are trying to find work, the lack of jobs in the market can be very dispiriting. I want you to tap into the emotional excitement of transforming that feeling.

I have spent many, many years helping people find new jobs and change careers. The very first business I set up, Alexander Mann, was a recruitment agency. I still love that buzz of matching someone to a job that is right for them but also finding a person who will add value to the position and the new company. In fact, I wrote a whole book about the subject. It's called *Get The Job You Really Want*.

One of the key points I made in that book was how important it is to prove your value to a new employer. In tough economic times companies want to know a new person is a cost worth paying.

Always aim to demonstrate your value. Keep that in mind whenever you are writing an application letter or putting a CV together. Look for clues in the wording of the ad. Is there something in there you can show you have done?

If it's a sales job, have you recently made a particular sales target? If so, how much higher was it than the previous target? Or have you come up with a tweak to one particular process or system that's significantly helped reduce your company's costs? Can you show how that improved the performance of the team you're in?

If you are thinking about changing your career, the need to prove your value in a different sort of workplace is even more vital. Don't rush in. You may need to spend time re-training first. I am always impressed whenever I look at a CV and see that somebody has actively been improving their skills.

Change does create opportunities, but do consider the long-term impact. You might have to uproot your home and family, or end up commuting a long distance. If you're happy with that, great. However, you could turn the whole idea on its head. Instead of leaving your company, re-invent yourself inside it.

Perhaps you have been in the same job for a while, maybe reasonably happy. What you've noticed, though, is that other people are getting promoted, not you. That usually means your set of skills may be out of line with what is needed. If it's appropriate for the kind of work you want to do, think especially about boosting your computer and IT skills, which are so central to many jobs.

The message here is, again, get the experience and skills you need. Don't keep quiet and wonder, 'What if?' Tell your bosses you are interested in moving the company forward. Could you sit in and observe some meetings in a different part of the business? Can you spend time in the department you *are* interested in?

In any job search, use the power of the internet. Look on the online job boards. Use it to check out a company you are going to see. Usually you'll find something on its website about 'The Team'. There may be press articles about the person you'll be talking to. It's all great background for you to build on. There are also plenty of online courses for improving your skills.

The other option is to go off and set up a new business. If you have never started a business, then don't think it's not possible.

Let me finish off the story about my sister. Here she was, a housewife with three kids, who never wanted to be a businesswoman. Nazima happened to be a very good cook. Her samosas were already selling like hot ... samosas. My idea was she should get some larger cooking facilities. She told me, 'Don't be so ridiculous, James, I'm a housewife, how do I know how to do that?'

I said, 'What's the difference between that and doing it at home? You have got a little cooker. I am just saying, "Get a bigger cooker."'

Then she said she didn't have enough money. I had to work really hard to persuade her to let me provide some funding. She really didn't want me to, because she was worried she'd lose my money. I pointed out that I never had any guarantees as a Dragon. I am always risking my money. I would rather risk it with her, because I believed in her. 'Rather than pay me interest,' I said, 'just give me some samosas!' Finally she said, 'OK.'

Nazima did it. She found a unit, hired four of the mums she knew, and in the first month they made 10,000 samosas. Then she went to all the local shops, presented her samosas, and the shops were buying from her. Even I was sur-prised ... One of the mums mentioned that her husband was in the catering business. He came in on the selling side. It was the power of networking in action again. To cut a long story short, Nazima now has a whole range of samosas, spring rolls and kebabs and supplies hundreds of corner shops and retail outlets around the country.

Look at the way Nazima fought against the very idea of starting up a business. She came up with all the reasons why she couldn't do it. Yet once she had set her mind on it, she stuck with it. She had a product people really liked: they wanted to buy her samosas. She got the pricing right. She didn't try to do it alone and brought in a good team of people to help her. She proved that if you get the basics right the rest will follow.

And one final lesson I have learnt about starting up a business. I meet people all the time who tell me, 'I would love to be an entrepreneur, but I can't think of the next big idea.' They believe they have to invent something that nobody else has come up with.

My message is: you don't have to think of the next big idea. You don't have to be the next James Dyson. Take an existing concept and modify it. Look at McDonald's. Did they invent the hamburger? No. They did it cheaper and faster.

Did EasyJet invent airline travel? No. Stelios Haji-Ioannou created a solution that was easier and cheaper to use.

Most of the people I personally consider to be entrepreneurial geniuses have done the same. Something as simple as changing a name, adjusting a price point, tweaking a colour. That is just as forward-thinking as a new invention. In fact, to me, those people are even smarter than the inventors because they haven't had to invest ten years of research and development. As an investor I am always more likely to invest in those people than take a massive risk on something untried and untested.

Career change: the JC approach

- For a new job, make sure you can show real evidence of what you can do. Empty promises do not add value. Bring real proof of your skills.

- Think about staying with your current company, but really making a difference there. Re-train and re-launch your prospects.

- If you have the drive and passion, think about setting up a new business. A recession might be the best time to do just that.

- **You don't have to be a great inventor. Look at an area you can understand and make sure you do it better, faster, cheaper.**

7

Reveal Your Best

Presenting with confidence

You've just heard you've got a first interview for a new job. Or maybe you are going along to see a business adviser at the bank because you'd like them to give you a loan to start up a café in the local park. Or you are about to stand up in front of the local residents' association and propose yourself as chairperson.

In all of those potentially life-changing situations you want to be able to present well. And the confidence to present well comes from one thing. That is preparation, preparation, and some more preparation. The next meeting, the next interview, could transform your life. Why risk losing that opportunity by not thinking about the impression you make?

First of all, I always say don't take any risks with your personal presentation. People seem to think this is a rather old school approach. I actually disagree. If you look good, if you are smart, you immediately come across well. There is nothing to distract.

For an interview or an important meeting, I suggest a short checklist. Go through every aspect. Think about your clothes, hair, fingernails and shoes. What briefcase or bag are you going to take? It's all in the detail.

Make sure you are in tune with the people you are going to see. If it's a job at Google or Virgin you probably don't want the pin-stripes. If you are visiting the bank, a smart suit is always the best bet.

Do the basics well. Give the person you are meeting a good, straight handshake. Make sure it's not too bone-creaking, limp or sweaty! Make eye contact. Sit up. Sometimes people get over-concerned about the business plan or the job spec and forget the simple niceties.

Look for a way of connecting with them on a personal level. There might be a picture on their desk you can talk about. Maybe it's a photo of them finishing a ten-kilometre run. Ask them how it went. Perhaps there's an award for Employee of the Month on the wall. Again ask them what they did that caught the company's attention.

Try something a little bit left-field. Imagine I am a bank manager. You've come along to see me and pitch me a proposal. 'Oh, by the way,

James,' you say. 'It's ten o'clock. I wasn't sure if you'd had breakfast so I've brought a brownie along for you.' Somebody actually did that to me once, and I was quite impressed. And I ate the brownie!

Something so basic changes the dynamic. It breaks the ice, and relaxes the atmosphere. You will shine more strongly when you are less tense. If you have done your research you will be confident in the conversation. You don't want to dazzle the other person with knowledge. You want to have the knowledge at your fingertips, ready for when you need it.

I always find it helps to get in with an early question. If it's a job interview, ask what they think the key elements of the job are. That will tell you what they want you to tell them. Focus on those areas. Provide them with details on how you can help them improve those aspects.

During the interview, ask the interviewer as many questions as they are asking you. Any meeting is a two-way exchange of information. It's not about you sitting there being grilled. You also have the right to ask. The more you ask, the more information you can glean from which to answer their questions. If I have ever left a meeting and I have felt I haven't performed well, it's generally because it was a one-way meeting.

It's like going on a date. If at the end of the evening you've said nothing, you pretty well know they're not going to call you back. But if when you get home it feels like you said as much as she or he did, it's a lot more promising.

If you are feeling nervous, remember that everybody does. Don't worry too much about hiding any nerves. They can actually show just how much you really want the job or the loan. Being arrogant is not usually a plus point. Some gentle humour goes down well. On the other hand, don't turn up thinking you're the next Michael McIntyre. It's all about balance.

In the same way, if you do get fazed, take some time out. I once went to an important meeting that I thought was going to be one on one. When I walked into the room I found there was a whole panel waiting for me. It wasn't at all what I had been expecting and it certainly wasn't what I had been preparing for.

Rather than blundering on and getting flustered, I simply asked if I could visit the bathroom. Of course, they said. I used those few minutes to re-group and re-think my approach. When I walked back in I knew exactly what to expect and was ready to go.

I have another little trick I like to use after an interview or a meeting. As you get walked back to reception, ask, 'What's your gut feeling?' It's a beautiful, open-ended question. Because the formal meeting's over, you'll usually get an honest and useful answer.

They might say, 'You look like you'd fit in, but I'm not sure you've done enough direct work with clients.' That's something you can deal with immediately in a thank-you e-mail. A short thank-you note is always a good piece of follow-up. It's good manners, and reflects well on you. That's all part of good presentation.

Presenting: the JC approach

- Plan ahead. Don't run around in a panic ten minutes before you set out. Do plenty of research so you are confident in your answers.

- If at any point you feel you are not in control, take some time out. That will give you a chance to re-focus and get things back on track.

- Go in and play your full part in the conversation. Ask questions early and throughout. Make it a proper dialogue.

- Remember to get feedback with that simple 'What's your gut feeling?' question.

- **Great presentation comes from even greater preparation.**

8

Relationships Matter

Working with other people

My father passed on so many great pieces of advice to me. That in itself was a lesson, of course. The information you need to change your life is already out there, in other people's heads.

He was the one who taught me that successful business is not about good deals, but good relationships. My father was quite a philosophical person. Business, he told me, is about developing a relationship where you want to do business with that person again.

He showed me that it was really important in any deal to create a win-win position. Both people should come away feeling they have gained something. There are few things anyone has ever told me that have had more impact on me.

My father's view was that even if you came out on top, you should make the other person feel as if they had won. The way he put it was, 'Don't squeeze the last drop from the lemon.' That's a fantastic phrase, and so true.

The typical view is that to be successful, particularly in business, you have to be aggressive and ruthless. I don't see why. When people meet me, they often say they are surprised. I am quite soft-spoken. I do not get angry. I listen a lot.

There's no need to arm-wrestle everyone you meet. The person who is frustrating or not impressing me today might be a business partner tomorrow. When I was on *Dragons' Den*, even if somebody came in with what I thought was a crazy idea that I didn't want to invest in, I tried never to do them down. The secret is to respect other people's point of view. Embrace their differences. Treat them like human beings. You'll be surprised how someone you instinctively dislike might respond.

A few years ago I set up a school in Pakistan in memory of my father. After the Abdul Rashid Khan Campus opened, there were still many challenges ahead. We had to work out how to get kids from nearby villages to the school. The school was not near a city, so we had to attract teachers. The road needed strengthening for the rains of the monsoon season.

To help me I asked for advice from Seema Aziz, a successful businesswoman who advised the government on schooling. She took me on a tour of the schools. What stuck with me was that during the whole busy day, Seema knew the name of every teacher in each of her schools. Despite the demands of running a major fashion house, she had taken time to learn every single one of their names. That showed enormous respect for the teachers, and it was hardly surprising that they worked so hard for her and that the schools were doing so well.

You can only build relationships with people you have spent time getting to know. Whenever somebody new joins one of my companies, I always aim to create a useful induction phase for them. I know it can be daunting coming into a company on day one, feeling a bit of an outsider on that first Monday. So I'll ask them to go and meet the finance director, but rather than leaving them both to get on with a nice, but meaningless, chat, I will take the time to give the new person some ideas for the conversation: 'Ask him about this great deal we did two years ago.'

And I'll do the same in reverse, and talk to the finance director in advance. I know the new guy, I know exactly what it was about him that convinced me to offer him the job. So I can get the finance director to ask a question which will reveal those strengths. That way both of them walk away with something concrete, and they have learnt a little about what each of them is good at.

Just as you should build good relationships, you also need to weed out the people who try to put you down. The usual reason is that they are weak. They are afraid. They feel threatened by you. I have heard them called 'crazymakers'. That's a perfect description. If you let them get to you, you will lose the plot. They will have succeeded in their aims.

Avoid those people. You know you can't change them. They won't listen to reason. You have to bypass them. So if you can, find a way to get them out of your life or at least push them to the edges of it.

Building relationships: the JC approach

- Good relationships will help you in the long term. Don't see every contact with other people as a contest you have to win. Leave a little juice in the lemon!

- Respecting other people's differences means you can use those differences to your advantage. Sometimes respect is in the detail, like remembering names.

- Try to avoid the people who want to stop you succeeding. Remember, they are the weak ones. Sidestep them, ignore them and focus on your own plans and ambitions.

- On your own you might be good, but within a team you can be great.

- **Being able to build long, fruitful relationships is always valuable. When you are trying to change your life it's essential.**

9

Regime Change

Looking after yourself

I went for a regular health check a couple of years ago. The doctor I saw challenged me to re-think my daily routine.

When all the tests were over and done with, I asked him what advice he had for me. He told me he didn't have any. I was disappointed, a bit annoyed in fact. I was expecting at least some feedback. But he just said, 'What do you want me to tell you that you don't already know?'

He ran through my lifestyle at the time. I was working all hours. I wasn't eating correctly. I was usually eating very late at night. I certainly wasn't exercising enough. 'You know all of that already,' he said, 'but that doesn't make any difference. Because it's not important to you. Otherwise you'd have changed your lifestyle already.'

His words really struck home. I realized that only if I *was* bothered could I change. As a result I decided to get fitter and more focused.

I had enjoyed all the challenges of building up my businesses. It was great fun, but very, very hard work. There was constant pressure and stress. The success I had achieved came at a price, which up to then I had been prepared to pay. The doctor's words made me re-assess how long I could keep doing that.

I changed things around. Just a few simple things. I started eating more sensibly. I began to make time to work out. I lost weight. I felt so much fitter. That in itself was a motivation, because I felt great and I wanted to stay that way.

Generally I have become far more aware that to be able to do well, you need to be in good physical shape. If you are not healthy, if you are constantly drained and tired, you are ineffective. I recognize that I am starting to believe we are what we eat. Every illness in the modern world seems to be connected back to our food intake.

I haven't slackened off my work-rate noticeably. I still work seven days a week. Even on a weekend I might well start meetings at 9 a.m., if not before. Then I will have business commitments through to the evening.

It is demanding to maintain that pace, that focus and that concentration. I think of it like a car. If the engine isn't working, you aren't going anywhere. I've connected the two. I've said, 'If I am going to be successful as an entrepreneur, unless my engine is properly tuned, I can't fire on all cylinders.' Therefore I have to make an effort.

I have a trainer who comes three times a week. Sometimes when he is ringing the doorbell at 7 in the morning I really would prefer to have a lie-in. Would I love a full-on fry-up in the morning? Of course I would. But you know what? I have muesli, yoghurt and fruit instead, because it's the right thing to do.

Like so many things in this book, getting this right is even more critical at a time of change. If you are not functioning correctly you're on a dodgy wicket before you start. I have maintained my regime change and I don't particularly like it. I'd love to eat what I want. I'd love not to have to work out. However, I know if I don't do it, I won't have any energy. I will be tired and ratty. I won't make good decisions.

So I get up and answer that doorbell at 7 a.m. By the time I get to the office, I have had a great workout. I am alive, I am energetic. I am feeling really good. As I come in through reception I am sending out huge amounts of positive energy. I can see the guys in the office saying, 'What is he *on*?'

Like the advice from the doctor I went to see, this is not radical. Believe me, I'm not bringing out a fitness DVD for Christmas – Matt Roberts doesn't need to get worried just yet. I am not telling you anything you don't already know. The key message here is, if I can change my life-style anybody can.

The benefits on your ability to change your life will be noticeable. Not only do I make better decisions, but I pass on that good feeling. What would happen if I slouched in, a bit lethargic? Or if I moaned, 'Can't wait for Friday. . .' As a side-effect of me feeling better, I am projecting a more positive message. That goes back to what you can bring out of other people.

If you are healthier, and sleeping better, you will be more focused, sharper. You will use your time more effectively, and you will have a much more positive outlook. You will avoid the negative thinking that comes with being tired, and the vicious circle that sets up.

You will rarely find me wallowing in negativity and analysing events that have been and gone. So many people spend hours asking why something happened to them. Where does that get you? Nowhere fast. The reason I don't waste my time over-analysing history is because I can't change it. And if I can't change it, what's the point?

Yes, I will try to learn a lesson from whatever happens, but I will look forward to applying it to the future. Because what I can do is change the future. I can influence future events because they are created by me. I focus on going forward.

Lifestyle: the JC approach

- To tackle the challenges ahead, you need to feel fit and full of energy. Your decision-making will be much sharper.

- You already know the changes you need to make to your lifestyle. Think about the benefits they will bring.

- If you feel more energized, people will see that and respond to it. So you're not only doing this for yourself, you're doing it to inspire and enthuse other people too.

- It's true a healthy body fosters a healthy mind. Best of all, you can use them both working together to create a positive influence on your future.

- **There is one relationship you definitely need to nurture. That's the relationship with yourself.**

10

Reap the Rewards

Motivating yourself

I really believe in the importance of reward-ing yourself. I don't think many people realize how important this is. It is something very few people do.

I see this a lot in the new businesses I work with. The people who have set them up think, 'No, no, no, I mustn't take any money out.' My view is quite different. I want them to celebrate reaching each of their milestones.

I am not saying, 'Spend everything you've got.' What I am saying is that there have to be rewards along the journey. You are working hard. You are achieving your targets. You should give yourself something. If you give yourself nothing, the journey becomes much harder because you are not seeing any benefits. Make sure you give yourself something to look for-ward to when you achieve a target. Bonuses are there for a reason.

Let's say you've just set up a new business offering home-based fitness training. When you make your first £500, go out and treat yourself. Have a really good meal, buy yourself a new iPad. You don't have to go crazy, but all of a sudden you have a new iPad and you are feeling pretty good about yourself.

What is important is not the iPad itself, but where it came from. It came from what you have achieved. You have converted what you have done into something real, something tangible.

This is an area where I disagreed fundamentally with my father. He was the complete opposite. He didn't believe in that at all: his view was always, 'You've got to wait until the business is successful. Don't over-indulge. Don't be reckless.' He would tell me I should always put any money straight back into the business.

I used to think about this and say, 'Dad, I think you're wrong, because I *am* the business. If I am not motivated, the business won't ever make it. You're separating the business from me. I am saying we are one, and you have got to treat it as one.'

For me, it's the same principle whatever you are trying to achieve. You are the person who is going to make it work. I have also seen too many businesses go bust. I know there are entre-preneurs who have created a lot of wealth on paper and ended up left with nothing.

The most extreme example of rewarding myself was in the second year of my first business. We had set ourselves the target of making a profit of £100,000 and we actually made £400,000. I was sitting in a meeting with the finance guy looking at my accounts.

I thought to myself, 'I need a bonus.' So off I went to the Rolls-Royce showroom and ordered a Silver Spirit (the Phantom would have to wait a few more years). I was twenty-four years old. It was crazy. On one level the car was an over-the-top, obscene purchase. But relatively speaking, on the profits that we had made, it wasn't. It was a bonus.

Yet as crazy as it was, I am telling you that car had a massive impact on my motivation. Every time I got into the driving seat of that Rolls, I believed, 'If I carry on doing this, I could real-ize more of my dreams.' Rewarding yourself for each milestone spurs you on to the next one.

I still do it, to this day. I'll give myself a pat on the back. Just recently my company Hamilton Bradshaw had a particularly good September, and the weekend after I had the results I saw a pair of shoes I liked and decided to buy them. They just put a smile on my face.

What that reward is will be different for everybody. I realize how lucky I was to buy the car I wanted at twenty-four. The reward doesn't have to be so blatant.

In 2009 I went to Kibera in Kenya with Sport Relief. We visited one of the AIDS camps. I walked into a corrugated tin shed in this shanty town, and met a woman who was living there with eight kids. It was one room, no more than three metres square. There was no furniture, just a box. The only light was what filtered through the cracks in the ceiling.

The woman who lived there had this huge grin on her face. I was quite confused because while she was talking, my eyes were going round the room. I was trying to work out in my head how nine people could sleep in this room. Even if you were lying side by side you probably couldn't fit them all in.

I said to the interpreter, 'I'm not being rude, but could you ask her a question? She seems really, really happy. Why is she so happy?' He asked her. She said, 'There is a reason I am happy. I have been on the waiting list for this shed for eighteen months and we only got it three weeks ago.' It put everything into per-spective.

Rewards: the JC approach

- A reward for reaching a milestone doesn't have to be expensive, but should mean something to you. It will have real value for you because it represents an achievement.

- If you wait too long before rewarding yourself, the journey can feel much longer than it needs to, and you may never see the fruits of your labour.

- Each reward becomes another piece of motivation for what you want to achieve. It reminds you how good you'll feel when you reach the next milestone.

- **Recognize the importance of celebrating your success – it will help you to become consistently successful.**

Conclusion

Closing the circle

When I left home at sixteen, I broke my father's heart. In an Asian family like ours, the concept of a family business is immensely important. In his mind, there was no question that he wanted to see his son taking over the business he had built up with painstaking care. So when I rejected that idea, he must have felt I was rejecting him.

I told him I was going to do my own thing and he was devastated. The house was full of tension, and on the day I left I thought he would never forgive me. He certainly thought I was spoilt and mollycoddled and that I would be crawling back in a couple of weeks. My mother had saved up £30 for me and I left home with that in my pocket.

As I walked away from the house I was in tears, praying that someone from the family would run after me to fetch me back, but no one did. I walked as slowly as I possibly could, and still no one came, so by the time I reached the train station I thought to myself, I really am going to have to do this.

My father and I were both very proud people. I didn't go home for two years. Even when I had set up my first business and was dying to show him what I was doing, he said he didn't understand recruitment, that it was a crazy business and it would never work.

But when my second company, Humana International, had grown to 100 offices, we held a huge event at the very smart Dorchester Hotel in London, with a world map showing the location of each of the offices. As I was making the presentation, I looked out into the audience and saw my father with tears in his eyes. I don't think he ever thought I would make it to that level.

As I came off the stage, he embraced me and said, 'I am so proud of you. This means more to me than all the success I could have wished for.'

That was the moment I knew that I had succeeded in what I had wanted to achieve. It proved the value – in the best possible way – of the decision I had taken to change my life.

Quick Reads

Books in the Quick Reads series

Amy's Diary	Maureen Lee
Beyond the Bounty	Tony Parsons
Bloody Valentine	James Patterson
Buster Fleabags	Rolf Harris
The Cave	Kate Mosse
Chickenfeed	Minette Walters
Cleanskin	Val McDermid
The Cleverness of Ladies	Alexander McCall Smith
Clouded Vision	Linwood Barclay
A Cool Head	Ian Rankin
The Dare	John Boyne
Doctor Who: Code of the Krillitanes	Justin Richards
Doctor Who: I Am a Dalek	Gareth Roberts
Doctor Who: Made of Steel	Terrance Dicks
Doctor Who: Magic of the Angels	Jacqueline Rayner
Doctor Who: Revenge of the Judoon	Terrance Dicks
Doctor Who: The Sontaran Games	Jacqueline Rayner
A Dream Come True	Maureen Lee
Follow Me	Sheila O'Flanagan
Full House	Maeve Binchy
Get the Life You Really Want	James Caan
Girl on the Platform	Josephine Cox
The Grey Man	Andy McNab
Hell Island	Matthew Reilly

Lose yourself
in a good
book with *Galaxy*®

Curled up on the sofa,
Sunday morning in pyjamas,
just before bed,
in the bath or
on the way to work?

Wherever, whenever,
you can escape
with a good book!

So go on...
indulge yourself with
a good read and the
smooth taste of
Galaxy® chocolate.

Quick Reads

Fall in love with reading

Quick Reads are brilliantly written short new books by bestselling authors and celebrities. Whether you're an avid reader who wants a quick fix or haven't picked up a book since school, sit back, relax and let Quick Reads inspire you.

We would like to thank all our funders:

We would also like to thank all our partners in the Quick Reads project for their help and support:

NIACE • unionlearn • National Book Tokens
The Reading Agency • National Literacy Trust
Welsh Books Council • Welsh Government
The Big Plus Scotland • DELNI • NALA

We want to get the country reading

Quick Reads, World Book Day and World Book Night are initiatives designed to encourage everyone in the UK and Ireland – whatever your age – to read more and discover the joy of books.

Quick Reads launches on **14 February 2012**
Find out how you can get involved at www.**quickreads**.org.uk

World Book Day is on **1 March 2012**
Find out how you can get involved at www.**worldbookday**.com

World Book Night is on **23 April 2012**
Find out how you can get involved at www.**worldbooknight**.org

Quick Reads 📖

Fall in love with reading

Doctor Who
Magic of the Angels

Jacqueline Rayner

BBC Books

*'No one from this time
will ever see that girl again ...'*

On a sight-seeing tour of London the Doctor wonders why so many young girls are going missing. When he sees Sammy Star's amazing magic act, he thinks he knows the answer. The Doctor and his friends team up with residents of an old people's home to discover the truth. And together they find themselves face to face with a deadly Weeping Angel.

Whatever you do – don't blink!

A thrilling all-new adventure featuring the Doctor, Amy and Rory, as played by Matt Smith, Karen Gillan and Arthur Darvill in the hit series from BBC Television.

Quick Reads

Fall in love with reading

The Little One

Lynda La Plante

Simon & Schuster

Are you scared of the dark?

Barbara needs a story. A struggling journalist, she tricks her way into the home of former soap star Margaret Reynolds. Desperate for a scoop, she finds instead a terrified woman living alone in a creepy manor house.

A piano plays in the night, footsteps run overhead, doors slam. The nights are full of strange noises. Barbara thinks there may be a child living upstairs, unseen. Little by little, actress Margaret's haunting story is revealed, and Barbara is left with a chilling discovery.

This spooky tale from bestselling author Lynda La Plante will make you want to sleep with the light on.

Quick Reads

Fall in love with reading

Full House

Maeve Binchy

Orion

Sometimes the people you love most
are the hardest to live with.

Dee loves her three children very much, but now they
are all grown up, isn't it time they left home?

But they are very happy at home. It doesn't cost them
anything and surely their parents like having a full
house? Then there is a crisis, and Dee decides things
have to change for the whole family . . . whether they
like it or not.

Quick Reads 📖

Fall in love with reading

Beyond the Bounty

Tony Parsons

Harper

Mutiny and murder in paradise …

The Mutiny on the Bounty is the most famous uprising in naval history. Led by Fletcher Christian, a desperate crew cast sadistic Captain Bligh adrift. They swap cruelty and the lash for easy living in the island heaven of Tahiti. However, paradise turns out to have a darker side …

Mr Christian dies in terrible agony. The Bounty burns. Cursed by murder and treachery, the rebels' dreams turn to nightmares, and all hope of seeing England again is lost forever …

Quick Reads 📖

Fall in love with reading

The Cleverness of Ladies

Alexander McCall Smith

Abacus

There are times when ladies must use
all their wisdom to tackle life's mysteries.

Mma Ramotswe, owner of the No.1 Ladies' Detective Agency, keeps her wits about her as she looks into why the country's star goalkeeper isn't saving goals. Georgina turns her rudeness into a virtue when she opens a successful hotel. Fabrizia shows her bravery when her husband betrays her. And gentle La proves that music really can make a difference.

With his trademark gift for storytelling, international bestselling author Alexander McCall Smith brings us five tales of love, heartbreak, hope and the cleverness of ladies.

Quick Reads 📖

Fall in love with reading

Quantum of Tweed:
The Man with the Nissan Micra

Conn Iggulden

Harper

Albert Rossi has many talents. He can spot cheap polyester at a hundred paces. He knows the value of a good pair of brogues. He is in fact the person you would have on speed-dial for any tailoring crisis. These skills are essential to a Gentleman's Outfitter from Eastcote. They are less useful for an international assassin.

When Albert accidentally runs over a pedestrian, he is launched into the murky world of murder-for-hire. Instead of a knock on the door from the police, he receives a mysterious phone call.

His life is about to get a whole lot more interesting . . .

Quick Reads

Fall in love with reading

Amy's Diary

Maureen Lee

Orion

A young woman finds her way
in a world at war.

On 3rd September 1939 Amy Browning started to write
a diary. It was a momentous day: Amy's 18th birthday
and the day her sister gave birth to a baby boy. It was
also the day Great Britain went to war with Germany.

To begin with life for Amy and her family in Opal Street,
Liverpool, went on much the same. Then the bombs
began to fall, and Amy's fears grew. Her brother was
fighting in France, her boyfriend had joined the RAF and
they all now lived in a very dangerous world …

Other resources

Enjoy this book? Find out about all the others from
www.quickreads.org.uk

Free courses are available for anyone who wants to develop
their skills. You can attend the courses in your local area.
If you'd like to find out more, phone 0800 66 0800.

For more information on developing your skills in Scotland
visit www.**thebigplus**.com

Join the Reading Agency's Six Book Challenge at
www.**sixbookchallenge**.org.uk

Publishers Barrington Stoke and New Island
also provide books for new readers.
www.**barringtonstoke**.co.uk • www.**newisland**.ie

The BBC runs an adult basic skills campaign.
See www.**bbc**.co.uk/**skillswise**

JAMES CAAN

GET THE JOB YOU REALLY WANT

'It is possible to have the job of your dreams. Together we are going to set about getting you there.

Before I joined the BBC's *Dragons' Den*, I spent thirty years setting up and running recruitment companies, placing hundreds of thousands of candidates in the jobs they really wanted.

I will take you through the process step by step. How to stay **positive** in a difficult economic climate and find the right opportunities. How to **package** yourself to make sure you secure an interview. The vital importance of **preparation**, so that you are relaxed and give a great **performance** at interview. How to show your **passion**, and ask the **perfect** questions. And finally, how to use your **power** by closing the best deal on a job offer.

At every stage I will help you rethink the traditional, formulaic approach to job hunting. It's the detail that makes the difference.

This book is not about hoping you get lucky. It is about creating your own luck.'

James Caan

'Really great, useful advice. I'm a fan' Sahar Hashemi, founder of Coffee Republic and author of *Anyone Can Do It*

'Simply brilliant. This practical, no-nonsense book will help you land the job of your dreams' Bev James, Chief Executive, Entrepreneurs Business Academy

JAMES CAAN

START YOUR BUSINESS IN 7 DAYS

'Everybody wants to be an entrepreneur. Every single day of my life I am bombarded by people with pitches. But 90% of new businesses fail, because their founders failed to ask themselves the simplest of questions.

I can save you years of wasted time and thousands of pounds of wasted money by giving you the ammunition to ask the right questions, and helping you make the decision that is right for you.

I will show you how to spend a maximum of seven days deciding if your idea is workable and bankable. How to say "I'm in", but equally importantly, to have the courage to say "I'm out". How to become your own Dragon.

Each piece of advice in this book is based on my thirty years of starting businesses. You will find all the fundamental ingredients for any new company, whatever sector you want to be in, whatever size of business you have in mind, along with the tools to make it work.

Answer all the tough questions I am going to get you to ask yourself and you will have a business that genuinely has a chance of success. You can be one of the 10% of businesses that do make it.'

James Caan